Citizenship and PSHE
Book 4

Contents

Deena Haydon
Pat King
Christine Moorcroft

Personal development

Raymond is five years old.
His sister Rita is twelve.

Raymond likes to get himself washed and dressed for school.

1. Who helps Raymond in this story? How?

2. Redraw and rewrite the story, showing Raymond at your age.

3. Make a time line to show your growing independence since you were five years old.

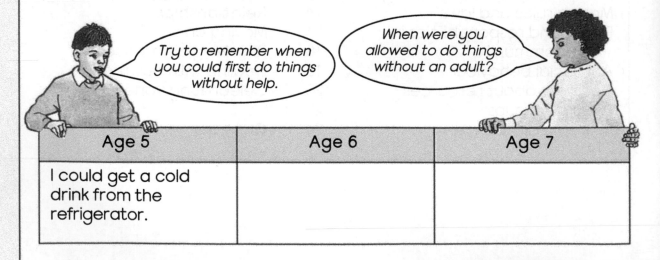

Age 5	Age 6	Age 7
I could get a cold drink from the refrigerator.		

4. How do you think the people who look after you feel when you go out or do things without them?

Useful words

anxious	proud
happy	relieved
left-out	responsible
not needed	worried

5. Why is Matt not allowed to go out with his friends?
   How might his father feel?

6. Why does Matt not want an adult to take him and his friends to Southport?

7. In a group, plan an ending for the story. It should make everyone feel happy.

8. What do you think children of your age should be allowed to do without an adult? Record your ideas and those of the class or group. Make a table.

Activity	For (✓)	Against (✗)
Go to the shops		
Travel by bus to town		
Travel to school		

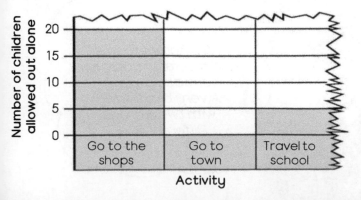

9. Use the table to make graphs showing what the group or class thinks.

What do most children in your class feel they should be allowed to do?

3

Indarjit will soon leave his primary school to go to the high school. His older sister and friends have told him a bit about his new school.

Science laboratories

A trampoline

French

Bonjour. Ça va?

The orchestra

School trips abroad

SUPER TOURS

A different room and a different teacher for each subject. A very big building with two storeys. Different rules.

1. With a partner, discuss the ways in which Indarjit's high school will be different from his primary school.

2. List the new things he might look forward to.
List any worries he might have.

3. In a group, brainstorm all the things you think you might find difficult when you change schools.

4. Talk to a partner about why you might find it difficult.

5. Consider one of these difficulties.
With a partner, plan a way to find out more about it.

All in a day's work

Holly is a sales manager for a company that sells and fits windscreens.

Holly's day at work

8:15   Drive to depot.

9:00   Arrive at depot. Greet salespeople.

9:15   Lead sales meeting. Discuss how well sales targets are being achieved; new targets; new incentives to earn bonuses; sales techniques; forward planning.

12:00   Lunch with salespeople.

1:00   Planning afternoon's visits, beginning with furthest away, working back towards depot, so that no time is wasted.

1:10   Drive to first call: customer who might benefit from more information.

2:00   Drive to next call: new contact. Explain company services and costs and what can be done for the client.

3:00   Drive to next call: customer who has problem with company service. Discuss problem. Find ways to solve it so that customer stays with the company.

4:00   Drive to depot. Telephone to make appointments for next day. Key in notes from each of the day's calls. Key in notes from morning sales meeting. Send them to salespeople and sales director.

6:00   Drive home.

Ian is a service engineer for a telecommunications company.

Ian's day at work

8:15   Begin work at home: check on palmtop computer what calls need to be made. List calls in order of times by which they must be done. Organise them according to locations.

9:00   Drive to first call: repair connection to customer's phone. Write up activity sheet for the work. Key the job code into palmtop computer.

9:30   Drive to next call: tune customer's television. Write up activity sheet. Key job code into computer.

10:00   Drive to next call: customer has complained about quality of reception on her television. Need to calm customer, explain how problem happened and what company is doing to put it right. Write up activity sheet. Key job code into computer.

10:30   Drive to next call: repeat visit to solve problem with telephone that keeps disconnecting. Find out why: fault is in the cabinet at end of road. Explain to customer how fault will be put right. Customer still unhappy. Write up activity sheet. Key job code into computer. Using computer, fax message to office to request call from senior engineer.

11:00   Continue calls.

12:00   Lunch with field manager to discuss any problems. Discuss problem of faulty telephone cabinet.

12:30   Continue calls.

5:30   Fax to office to confirm all jobs completed.

1. List the skills that Holly and Ian use in their work.

Give examples of when they use these skills.

Make a table.

Holly		Ian	
Skill	Example	Skill	Example
Driving	Drove to the depot Drove to appointments		

Find out about the skills that people you know use in their work.

 2. Circle the skills used by both Holly and Ian.
Which of these skills would be useful in other jobs?
Copy and complete the table.

Skill	Jobs
Driving	

 3. What kind of work do you think you might do in the future?
Which skills will be useful in this work?

 With a partner, discuss what you can already do that will help you to develop these skills.
What else do you need to learn?

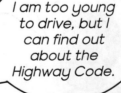

I am too young to drive, but I can find out about the Highway Code.

 4. Find out how you can learn this.

1. How did the people in the picture-story feel:
   - before they met?
   - in picture **a**?
   - in picture **b**?

2. With a partner, discuss what the jogger and the dog-walker could have said and done to put forward their point of view without being offensive.

How could they have learned more about each other's opinions?

How could they have avoided offending one another?

Useful words

angry
annoyed
bad-tempered
calm
cross
peaceful
placid
puzzled
relaxed
ruffled
serene
tranquil
unsettled
vexed

3. Rewrite the story as a dialogue.
Change it so that the people show respect for one another's opinions and feelings.

Your rewritten story should end with the two people understanding more about one another's opinions.

They might still disagree.

4. With a partner, write a set of rules for:

a. giving your opinion
b. respecting other people's opinions.

Think about:
- *making others want to listen to you*
- *understanding others' opinions*
- *feeling positive*
- *making others feel positive.*

5. Find out how people present their opinions in the media.

How well do they show respect for other people's points of view?
Copy and complete the table.

Name	Example	Marks out of 10

1. Rosie wants a new bike.
   With a partner, discuss Rosie's thoughts.

   Write about Rosie's thoughts in each picture.

   Copy and complete the table.

Useful words	
creative	hopeful
depressed	manipulative
disappointed	shrewd

Picture	Rosie's thoughts	How realistic is she being?	How positive is she being?
a			

Explain your answers.

2. What else could Rosie do?
   What are the advantages and disadvantages of each solution?

Think about time, people's feelings, being positive, and making plans.

3. With a partner, discuss the occasions when you have been given, or have earned, money.

   Make notes about these occasions.

My brother pays me for washing his car.

My gran gave me money for my birthday.

My dad gives me pocket money every Saturday.

4. On what do you spend your money?
   List the money you have been given this week.
   Add it up.

   List everything you have spent this week.
   Add it up.

5. How could you save?

6. Find out about different ways for children to save.

You could write to banks and building societies.

You could use the Internet.

How can you save money to buy what you want or need in the future?

11

It is not always easy to decide whether something is wrong.

1. Are the actions of Jo and Ali wrong?
   Does the amount of money make a difference?
   What do you think Jo and Ali should do?
   Explain your reasons.

2. Why might these children be thinking about stealing?

   Do you think it makes a difference if:

   a. they have never stolen before
   b. they are unfed and really hungry
   c. they are aged five, ten, or fifteen?

   Discuss your views with a partner.
   Do you agree?

citizenship

Sometimes we make judgements or form opinions based on information presented by others.

STATEMENT

I was walking home from school on Tuesday afternoon. A small group of teenagers ran out of the arcade and across the road laughing. One said, "That was a laugh. Let's go and have a joke with the woman at the petrol station."

HOME NEWS

CHILDHOOD IN CRISES
A special report

GANG PROBLEM RETURNS TO LOCAL SHOPPING ARCADE
By Emma Glastonbury

BOY 10 IN FEAR FOR HIS LIFE

3. This statement and the newspaper headlines are about the same event.
Do the headlines match the statement?
Can you tell if the teenagers really did anything wrong from the statement?
Do 'stories' or 'reports' always tell the whole story?

4. The media (newspapers, radio, TV, magazines, Internet) present information in certain ways to gain attention and interest.
Describe some of the methods used.

shock headline

special report covering issue of interest

Useful words

cartoons	photographs
diagrams	short quotes
features	soundbites
headlines	special reports
key words	

5. When trying to make a judgement, what do you need to think about?
Explain how people, and the media, can try to influence you by exaggerating, sensationalising, mixing fact and opinion, relying on 'hearsay' or memory.

Suspect A

He had curly blond hair, a long beard and wore a blue jumper, I think.

Evidence of witness X

What do you need to think about when forming an opinion or making a judgement?

Making rules and laws

What is the difference between **illegal** and **unconventional**?

1. Within one group, or community, people may do many things in the same way. They **conform**.
    List some ways in which people conform.

Group	Ways in which people conform
School	uniform for pupils rules agreed by each class

Think about clothes, food, language, homes and entertainment.

What a weirdo!

Look at that cool hairstyle!

2. Sometimes people choose to be different.
    In a group, discuss what others do when someone is 'different'.

3. Plan and write a poem about 'Being different'. Decide whether your poem is presenting the thoughts and feelings of the 'different' person, or the reactions of other people.

Poem planning table	
Line	Content
1	Introduce the character
2	His or her appearance
3	More about appearance
4	An action
5	Another action
6	What people do
7	What people say
8	Conclusion

4. Note five class or school rules.
   With a partner, discuss why these rules exist.
   Copy and complete the table.

Think about: safety, fairness, protection from harm, respect for others' property, the environment, accepting responsibility for words and actions.

Rule	Reason	Reward	Sanction	Agree/ change/ abolish?

What rewards do you receive for obeying these rules?
What sanctions are there for those who do not follow the rules?
Do you agree with each rule, think it should be changed or abolished?

5.

laws for roads

laws for property

laws about how we treat people

The 'Laws of the land' are usually rules developed for everyone living in a particular country.
Who makes laws? How?
Who **enforces** laws?
What might be the consequences for people who 'break the law'?

Useful words

Act of Parliament	guilty
caution	imprisonment
community	innocent
service	judge
conviction	jury
crime	offence
curfew	parliament
evidence	sentence
fine	witness

In what ways do you think the following issues make a difference?

a. Age.
b. First offence.
c. Previous convictions.
d. Reliability of evidence.
e. Motive.
f. Seriousness of the crime.
g. Being there, but not actually doing anything.

Using examples, explain your point of view.
Present it to the class. Do others agree?

Who is responsible for looking after your community?

1. Who is responsible for the places, people and services in your community?
   Who might solve any problems? How?

   Copy and complete the table.

Hello, I'd like to report...

Neighbourhood Watch Area

Place	Who is responsible?
roads park garden	
Services	
street lamps drains	

2. Identify a problem or issue in your community. For example, litter, dog fouling, heavy traffic, loud music from the pub at night, smell from nearby landfill site.

In small groups, think of some possible solutions.
How could you find out more?
Who could you involve?
How can you present your views to others?
What options do you have?

Pooper-Scooper Design Competition

3. Are you aware of any crimes regularly committed in your community?
Carry out a survey to find out what others know or believe.
You could include:

a. adults, children, teenagers
b. shopkeepers, businesses, residents
c. local councillors
d. public service providers.

Do they all talk about the same issues?
Can you suggest any crime prevention ideas?

Think about:
- types of crime
- people likely to commit crime
- reasons
- effects on others
- reactions of others
- prevention.

4. As well as responsibilities, people in communities have rights.

Find out about laws and conventions developed to make sure people are safe, healthy, protected from harm, treated fairly, respected, not discriminated against, and enjoy their own culture.

In what ways can you behave responsibly in your community?

Antisocial behaviour

Groups of people sometimes behave in an antisocial way.

1. What is happening in this picture?
   Why are some of the football supporters behaving like this?

2. Imagine you are a reporter for the 'Daily Blab'.
   You need to write an article about this incident.
   To prepare for this, you need to interview various people, such as the residents, supporters at the bus stop, the shopkeeper, the publican, the hooligans, and the police.

In a group or pair, write down what you think each of these people would say if you asked the following questions:

Think of some other questions – you may find the worksheet 'Points of view' helpful.

3. Write a summary for the newspaper article.
   You may add your own views.
   Compare and discuss the newspaper articles produced by the class.

4. Newspapers sometimes tell us about other sorts of antisocial behaviour carried out by groups.

Think about events you know of in your community or elsewhere.
Why do people behave in this way?

What would you do if you were in a group that started to behave in an antisocial way?

Decisions about resources

At the Supermall, we offer the ideal shopping experience. Leave your car in the safety of our supervised, free car park. Buy food, clothes, shoes, household items galore from our huge range of shops and boutiques. Meet, and eat any type of food in one of our exclusive cafes or restaurants. Relax and enjoy a film at the multi-screen cinema. At last, shopping can be enjoyable, and not a chore.
'Whatever the weather, whatever your needs, you'll find just what you need at the Supermall.'

SOS – Save Our Shops
Serving the local community for more than 50 years, the shops in Sutton Street provide just what you want. Locally produced fruit and veg, bread and cakes are served by friendly, helpful shopkeepers who know their customers' names and serve with a smile – whether in the shop or delivering to your home. On your doorstep, these shops are at the heart of our community.

1. List the advantages put forward for shopping:

   a. at the Supermall
   b. at the local shops

   Are there any disadvantages?
   Copy and complete the table.

Think about:
- *needs of different people or groups*
- *travel, cost*
- *variety of choice*
- *employment*
- *traditions*
- *new opportunities.*

The Supermall		The local shops	
+	–	+	–
free parking	need to travel	within walking distance	

Many people make choices about what to buy based on information about:

Raw materials

organically
grown

solid oak or pine

long-life

natural
fibres

free-range

hand-crafted by
women's co-operative

Production

not tested
on animals

recycle this
container

newspaper

2. Write a report encouraging others to
   think about the effects of their choices.

3. What information has to be provided
   on a product?
   Does this influence your choice?

*Think about:
cost, lifespan,
animal welfare,
environment,
employment,
luxury, necessity,
individual and
community
welfare.*

4. Find out about organisations that:

   a. provide information
   for consumers

   b. try to influence
   consumer choice.
   Here are some examples:

Consumers'
Association

OXFAM; FRIENDS OF THE EARTH;
SUPERMARKETS;
HEALTH EDUCATION AUTHORITY;
VEGETARIAN SOCIETY; TRAIDCRAFT

1. How are people trying to change decisions or laws in these photographs?

2. As an individual, how would you try to change a decision you felt was unfair or wrong?

3. Some individuals are willing to give up or suffer a great deal for their beliefs and to bring about change.

   Find out about one of these people:
   ● Emmeline Pankhurst
   ● Nelson Mandela
   ● Chico Mendes
   ● Mahatma Gandhi
   ● Pat Arrowsmith
   ● Sojourner Truth.

Individuals may join a **pressure group** in which group members share the same beliefs and try to influence others.

Fox hunting: a national tradition

Fox hunting: a cruel 'sport'

Sometimes pressure groups want to keep things as they are.

Sometimes, they want to increase awareness about a particular issue and change the law.

4. In what ways do pressure groups **campaign** for their cause?

Presenting their views to local councillors.

Giving TV or radio interviews.

Information leaflets and posters.

Collect local newspapers and read the articles.
What pressure groups are mentioned?
What are they campaigning for?
How do they try to influence people?

Copy and complete the table.

Pressure group	Aims	Methods used
'Save Our Shops' group	encourage people to use local shops	posters public meeting petition for customers
Amnesty International		

Making a difference

Sometimes things happen in a local community that people don't like.

In the village of Martinvale, a company planned to build an incinerator for burning animal carcasses.

Some local people were very worried about this. They wanted to stop it. This is what they did.

Research	They found out as much information as they could about incinerators for burning carcasses and about who would make the decision.
Decided what to do	They formed a protest group and decided on their plan of action.
Took action	They gathered signatures on a petition, raised publicity, wrote to and visited the local council to present their case.

They made a difference. After a long time, the council decided not to allow the incinerator to be built.

1. The people in Martinvale were able to influence a decision.
    How could you make a difference?
    Think about something in your school or local community that
    you would like to change.
    Share your ideas in a group and then in the class.

Stop dogs making a mess on the school field.

Have something to do at playtime.

Put litter bins near the shops.

Have a healthy tuck shop.

Your teacher will help you decide what could be possible and how
long you will need.

2. For your chosen improvement, go through steps similar to those
    used by the people of Martinvale.
    Copy and complete the table.

Research the issue	Decide what needs to be done	Take action

You may find the worksheet 'Making a difference' useful.

3. How successful were you? What could you have done differently?

How does working with a group help you to make a difference?

Changes during puberty

Our bodies are full of systems!

You have 'systems' in your body. Each system does a job: the blood system, the breathing system, the digestive system, the nervous system ... .

These systems grow with you but do not change during puberty very much.
There is one system that changes when you are between nine and fifteen years old. This is the reproductive system that will enable you to produce babies.

Harry	Susie	Fawzia	Bill	Jane	Mary	David	Meera	Gobind
9	4	16	18	11	20	40	7	14

1. List the people in the picture whose reproductive systems could have developed enough to produce babies. Explain your answer.

2. List some of the changes in the reproductive system about which you know:
   ● in girls
   ● in boys.

Lifestyle

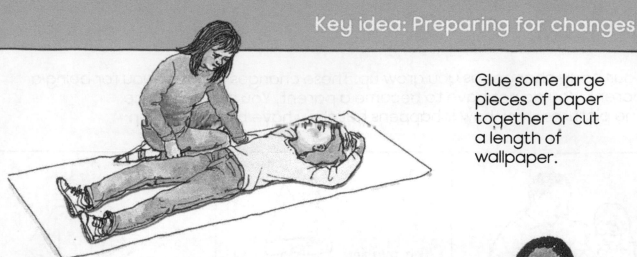

Glue some large pieces of paper together or cut a length of wallpaper.

Do not use ready-pasted wallpaper. The paste may contain a harmful fungicide.

3. Draw around a partner's outli

With a partner, decide where on the outline the body parts belong.
Label them in the correct place.
Highlight those that will change.

Be sensitive. Draw the shape 1cm from the body.

Body parts			
bladder	heart	lungs	testicles
brain	intestines	ovaries	trachea
breasts	kidneys	penis	uterus (womb)
gullet	liver	stomach	vagina

4. Which body parts belong to the reproductive system? Sort them into male and female.

5. Find out about the changes that will happen inside and outside your body.

Which changes are you looking forward to, and which changes worry you?

New baby

Your body changes as you grow up. These changes prepare you for being a parent. You do not have to become a parent. You have a choice.
The pictures show how it happens but they have been mixed up:

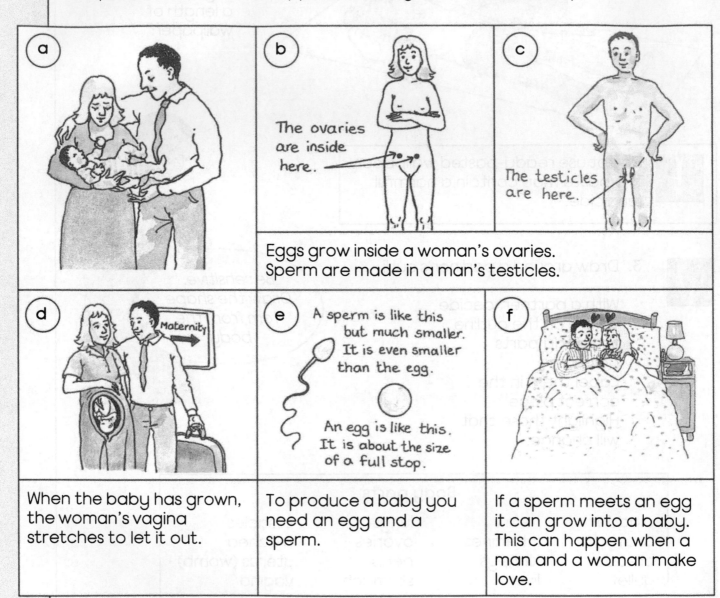

(a)

(b) The ovaries are inside here.

(c) The testicles are here.

Eggs grow inside a woman's ovaries.
Sperm are made in a man's testicles.

(d) Maternity →

(e) A sperm is like this but much smaller. It is even smaller than the egg.

An egg is like this. It is about the size of a full stop.

(f)

When the baby has grown, the woman's vagina stretches to let it out.

To produce a baby you need an egg and a sperm.

If a sperm meets an egg it can grow into a baby. This can happen when a man and a woman make love.

1. Re-order the pictures. Compare this with your partner's story.

2. List the things a couple should think about before they make love.

Having a baby is a big responsibility. People can usually decide if and when they want to have children.

Once your reproductive parts are mature you are **fertile**, but you have not finished growing. You could produce a baby.

TAKE CARE

Young person in charge of working reproductive parts!

3. Discuss this sign with your group. What might it mean?

4. At what age do you think people are ready for the responsibility of a baby? Copy and complete the table.

The best age groups for having babies (✔)								
	11–16	16–20	20–25	25–30	30–40	40–50	50–60	60+
Male								
Female								

Explain your answers.

5. Write a sentence for each picture. Describe how the people might feel about having children.

Think about people who have unplanned children.

6. Explain why some people choose to have children while others do not.

Why is being fertile a big responsibility?

Ken Gets Lost

a.

PETE THE PERSUADER PICKS ON PAULA

b.

The Group Goes Separate Ways

c.

The Stranger Tries to take Charge

d.

Sally Accepts a Lift

e.

1. Discuss these titles with your group. What might happen in each story?

2. Plan a story for one of the titles.

3. Explain why people sometimes do unsafe things.

4. Who is responsible for keeping you safe:
   ● at home
   ● in school
   ● in the community?

Characters	How the story begins.
Name Description	
The middle of the story: what happens.	
Two different endings: what they do, who they go to for help.	
1.	2.

In what ways are you responsible for your own safety?

Leah likes to talk to her gran. She trusts her and feels confident with her because Gran always listens to her.

5. Talk to a partner about Leah's problem.
How might Leah have felt before this picture?
How might she feel now?

If you feel unsafe or uncomfortable, it helps to talk to someone you trust. You need someone who will listen.

People who listen	People who do not listen
ask you to tell them what is worrying you	tell you to go away and say, 'Don't be silly'

6. Think about people who listen and people who do not listen to you.
What do they do?
What do they say?
Copy and complete the table.

Trust is ... when you know someone will keep your secrets.

7. Draw and describe a person you trust. Explain why you trust this person.

Trust is ... when you know someone will protect you.

8. What is trust?
With a partner, write some 'Trust is ...' sentences.
Decorate and display them.

How do you know whom to trust?

1. How might Mahmet feel in picture **b**?
   Explain your answer.

2. What might Mahmet do in picture **d**?
   Why?
   What might be the consequences?

3. What would you do?
   Why?

4. Were the children being good friends to one
   another and to Mahmet?

   Explain your answer.
   Compare and discuss your answer with others.
   Did you all agree?

Think about what influences you.

5. List some things that people try to persuade others to do.
Why do they do this?
What do they say to try to persuade people?

Think about times when people have tried to persuade you to do something you knew was wrong.

6. In a group, make up a short story about persuasion.

Use a storyboard to plan it.

Show different endings and **consequences** for the story.
Describe how the people feel.

Example, for Mahmet's story:

Storyboard	
Mahmet, Janey, Michael and Zara are wondering what to do. They feel bored.	Someone suggests playing by the railway. They feel excited.
Mahmet refuses because it is dangerous. He feels silly when the others laugh at him.	They begin walking towards the railway. Mahmet ...

Not for me. I'll see you tomorrow.

I'd rather ... .

Wouldn't you prefer to ... .

7. With your group, list things you can do and say if someone tries to persuade you to do something you do not want to do.

8. Find out where you can get help if you find it difficult to cope with pressures:
   - at home
   - at school
   - in the community.

What can you do if someone tries to persuade you to do something you feel is wrong or silly?

Different things worry and frighten Sara and Andy.

1. Sort Sara's and Andy's worries using a chart.

   Make another table to show things that worry or scare you.

Sara's worries	
People	
Places	
Real things	
Imaginary things	
Things that might happen	

Feeling safe can mean different things to different people.

2. Make a 'feeling safe' display to show the feelings of your group.

Feeling safe is being tucked up in a warm bed.

Feeling safe is being indoors during a thunderstorm.

Feeling safe is being with my grandad.

3. With a partner, discuss the effects that fears and worries can have on people.

Copy and complete the table.

Think about the feelings caused by fears or worries.

What might these feelings cause children to do?

Worry or fear	Feelings	What the person might do

Harry is worried because his parents are splitting up. He doesn't want to go to school in case his dad isn't at home when he gets back.

Mia is worried because her sister is in hospital. She is scared that her sister might die. Mia won't talk to anyone.

4. Information can help people to cope with fears and worries. What information might help Mia and Harry? Who could they talk to about their concerns and feelings?

For example, it might help Mia if she knew more about her sister's illness.

5. For each of the fears or worries on your chart, list the kind of information that might help.

6. Where can people get this information?

If you had a fear or worry, what could you do that would help you to cope with it?

Drugs

Drugs are chemicals that affect your body or your mind.

1. In a group, list the things that might be in the box Tony and Samantha have found.
   List any drugs you can think of.
   Compare lists with other groups.

2. Sort the drugs on your list into sets.
   The headings on the table may help, but you may think of others.

Medicines		Legal, but not medicines			Illegal
No prescription	Prescription only	For anyone	Over 16	Over 18	

3. Check your answers with your teacher.
   Your teacher may add some drugs to your list, or suggest altering your table.

Describe any changes your teacher made that surprised you.

Some drugs are used as medicines by people who need treatment. Some people may use these and other drugs to alter their mood. They like the way the drugs make them feel.

4. What makes Kirsty and Jamie decide to try taking drugs?

   Describe how they felt in picture a.
   What dangers might there be?

5. Why might the others have offered drugs to Kirsty and Jamie?

6. Finish the story.

7. Rewrite the story, showing what might have happened if Kirsty and Jamie had said 'No' to the drugs.

   Use thought bubbles to show their feelings.

Use pictures, speech and thought bubbles.

8. Why might people take drugs in the first place?
   Why might they continue to take them even when their health suffers?

What would you do if someone offered you drugs?

Beating the bugs

'Bug' is a word people sometimes use for a bacterium or virus that makes them ill.

1. In the pictures, how could bacteria or viruses cause illnesses or infections?

   What could the children have done to reduce the risk of spreading illnesses or infections?

   Copy and complete the table.

Picture	How bacteria and viruses spread	What the children could have done
a		
b		

> Bacteria and viruses can get into the body in different ways (for example, through the air we breathe, from contaminated water, if infected blood gets into the body).

2. With a partner, make a list of illnesses and infections.
   Write what you know about how they are passed from one person to another.

3. Research an illness or infection caused by a bacterium or virus.

What causes the illness or infection?	How does the bacterium or virus get into the body?	What can people do to reduce the risk of infection or illness?	How can people with the illness or infection try not to pass it on to others?

Use these sources:

The Internet

4. In your group, prepare a presentation about the illness or infection you have researched.

Use the presentation to inform the rest of the class.

You could:
● make posters
● write and draw overhead transparencies
● enact a short play
● perform a poem.

How can you reduce the risk of infection from bacteria and viruses in yourself and others?

Moving on

In some places, children move to a new school when they are 11 years old.

Sarah   Mel   Anna

Sarah, Mel and Anna have been in the same class since they started school at the age of four.

Today they are setting out for their new schools. Their parents have decided on different schools, so they won't be together.

 1. How might the girls feel about going to their new schools?

Copy and complete the table.

Positive feelings	Negative feelings
Look forward to new lessons.	Worried they won't know anyone.

2. How might going to different schools affect the girls' friendship? Do you think they will still be friends by the end of the first year? Why?

What could they do to help maintain their friendship?

Arrange a regular time together each week?

Set out for school together?

Join a weekend club together?

3. In their new schools, they will make new friends. How might this make their old friends feel?

Sometimes we forget that we can keep old friends as well as making new ones.

Anna   Sarah   Becky   Esther

How can Sarah make Anna feel she is still valued as a friend? What might make Anna feel rejected? How could Anna help the situation?

Resolving differences

People who live close to one another sometimes have disagreements.

1. How can you tell that these people are angry and arguing?

2. Make up a conversation for the argument.

   If you want to include rude words, don't write them, put ***** instead.

> What could the argument be about? How could it be sorted out?

To sort out an argument, people can **compromise** and **negotiate**.

3. Using a dictionary, find out what these words mean.

4. Find out what **mediate** means.
   Who could mediate in the argument shown here?

5. Look for **compromises**, **negotiation** and a **mediator** in this story.

Copy and complete the table.

	Picture	Person	How?
Compromise			
Negotiation			
Mediator			

6. Think about a time when you used compromise, negotiation or mediation to sort out a disagreement. What did you do to make it successful?

7. There are organisations that act as mediators between people or countries who disagree or fight. Find out the name of an organisation that does this. What is its role?

What skills are needed to be a good mediator?

Dealing with bullying

 1. Talk to a partner about what is happening in these pictures. Is it bullying? What do you think 'bullying' means?

 2. Write the story of each picture. Explain what is happening. Draw and write what you think happened in picture **d**.

 Write an ending for the story.

3. Describe the feelings of the boy who ran away:
   ● in pictures **a** to **d**
   ● later that day
   ● the next morning before school.

Sometimes people say or do one thing but they think or feel something else.

 4. Write a list of words to describe how the other three boys felt.

They may have a mixture of feelings.

 5. Write down what you think they might be saying. Is this the same as their feelings?

Why might they think one thing but say another?

You could use speech and thought bubbles.

Useful words
scared
strong
guilty
feeling of power

6. In a group, list some examples of bullying:
   - in school
   - at home
   - in the local community.

There are many kinds of bullying.

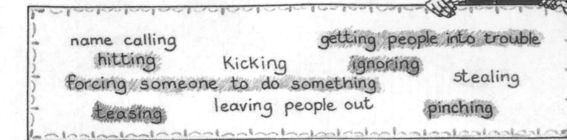

name calling   getting people into trouble
hitting   Kicking   ignoring
forcing someone to do something   stealing
teasing   leaving people out   pinching

7. Why do people bully others?
   Think of at least three reasons.
   The ideas below may help.

A bullied person may feel angry, upset, scared, frightened to tell anyone. He or she may want to hurt someone else.

Someone who bullies others may feel scared, lonely, unhappy, big, powerful, strong, in need of friends.

8. How can you help children who bully and children who are bullied in your school?
   Copy and complete the table.

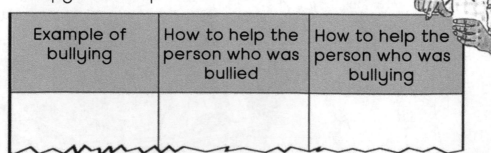

The planning table may help.

Example of bullying	How to help the person who was bullied	How to help the person who was bullying

What responsibility does the rest of the class or school have to stop bullying?

45

The Chan family is moving to a new town because Mr Chan has a new job.
They have been very happy in Mayfield Close and have many friends there.

Your **culture** includes your beliefs, customs and the way you live. These are sometimes based on your religion.

1. What can you see in the picture that suggests the families in Mayfield Close are from different cultures?

Find out about some of the cultures represented in Mayfield Close.

The colour of a person's skin is not a good guide to their culture.

Although people may appear to be from a particular culture, we must take care not to **stereotype** them. We may judge people by appearances but we don't know what they are really like.

2. The people in Mayfield Close are good friends. Although their cultures are different, they have many things in common.

I play chess.

So do I. Let's have a game.

So do I.

I'll show you how to cook it.

I really enjoy Indian food.

I'm trying to grow some vegetables.

I'll help you. I've done a lot of gardening.

I've got a new computer game.

Let's have a go!

In what ways do you think the people in Mayfield Close are similar?

3. It is important to respect other people's cultures. Imagine you are moving to Mayfield Close. How could you show respect for the various cultures of the families in the street?

Think about finding out what may upset or worry them, what they may enjoy.

Glossary

antisocial (18)   Causing offence or harm to other people.

bacterium (38)   (plural bacteria) A microscopic living organism.

bladder (27)   The sac in which urine, produced in the kidneys, collects.

campaign (23)   Organised activities for a particular purpose or goal.

carcass (24)   The remains of a dead animal.

conform (14)   To follow rules, customs or ways of doing things.

consequence (33)   Something that occurs as a result of something else.

contaminate (38)   To pollute with poisonous or harmful substances.

convention (17)   An accepted way of doing things or an agreement between countries to obey the same law.

dialogue (9)   A written or spoken conversation between two individuals or groups of people.

drug (36)   A material used as a medicine, to cure or prevent illness or as a painkiller. A material that some people take to alter their state of mind.

enforce (15)   To make something happen.

fertile (29)   Having a mature reproductive system (able to produce babies).

illegal (14)   To break the law.

incentive (6)   A reward or payment of some kind to encourage people to do something.

incinerator (24)   A furnace for burning rubbish and waste material.

infection (38)   A **contamination** caused by a germ or **virus**.

issue (15)   An important topic of discussion or interest.

kidneys (27)   A pair of organs in the body in which urine (waste liquid from the digestive system) is produced.

medicine (36)   A drug taken to treat an illness or infection.

offensive (8)   Causing hurt feelings or anger.

ovaries (27)   A pair of organs, in females, in which ova (eggs) are produced.

prescription (36)   A form filled in by a doctor asking a pharmacist to sell or give medicine to someone.

puberty (26)   The time when the reproductive organs become mature (able to produce babies).

sanction (15)   A penalty for disobeying a rule or law.

stereotype (47)   Images or assumptions that imply that all people of a particular group are the same.

technique (6)   A way of doing something.

testicles (27)   A pair of organs, in males, in which sperm are produced.

trachea (27)   The tube that carries air from the throat to the lungs.

unconventional (14)   Unusual, not what normally happens.

virus (38)   A microscopic living organism, smaller than a bacterium, which can breed only in living cells.